ANCESTRAL HEALING
for Your Spiritual and Genetic Families

ANCESTRAL HEALING
for Your Spiritual and Genetic Families

Jeanne Ruland and Shantidevi

EARTHDANCER

AN INNER TRADITIONS IMPRINT

First edition 2020, reprinted 2022

Jeanne Ruland and Shantidevi
Ancestral Healing for Your Spiritual and Genetic Families

This English edition © 2020 Earthdancer GmbH
English translation © 2019 JMS books LLP
Editing by JMS books LLP (www.jmseditorial.com)

Originally published as: *Aumakua – Segen und Potenzial unserer Wurzeln*
World © 2013 Schirner Verlag, Darmstadt, Germany

Cover design: DesignIsIdentity.com
Cover photography: Fominayaphoto/shutterstock.com
Cover illustration: kurbanov/shutterstock.com
Typesetting and layout: DesignIsIdentity.com
Typeset in Minion and Meta Plus

Printed and bound in China by Midas Printing Ltd.

ISBN 978-1-64411-034-8 (print)
ISBN 978-1-64411-035-5 (ebook)

Published by Earthdancer, an imprint of Inner Traditions
www.earthdancerbooks.com, www.innertraditions.com

MIX
Paper from
responsible sources
FSC
www.fsc.org
FSC® C169962

Dedications

I would like to dedicate this small book to the ALOHA SPIRIT
and the AUMAKUA, the ancestors, who came before us and
prepared our path.

Jeanne Ruland

* * *

I dedicate this small book to the one power, the great love that
creates and maintains us and that is our true being. Love
leads us toward experience and blesses all that exists. Love is
the greatest creative force, and we live through love. Love
is the strongest healing power in the universe, leading us on
our own very individual spiritual path and ultimately bringing us home into our true being.

Shantidevi

Contents

Acknowledgements by Jeanne Ruland

I would like to thank my paternal grandparents with all my heart. They always believed in and supported me; they carried me, protected me, and encouraged and helped shape me. They were always there for me, giving me love, a sense of security, and the courage to follow my own path in life and live the way I was born to live. Thank you for all the love that I was privileged to experience because of you.

I bless the other ancestors whose blood has commingled in my veins and I thank my parents for giving me the life that I have taken into my own two loving hands. I pass the love that I have experienced and that lives within me to my children so that all those who come after me may have a part of it. I bless you.

I would like to thank my AUMAKUA, my spiritual ancestors, who are part of my OHANA, my family. I have a connection to the powers of the Earth and of the universe, and I thank the whole line of my spiritual ancestors for all the initiations, deep inner experiences, and insights that have illuminated my path and forged a link to my spiritual powers and abilities, my true heritage. I honor and bless my spiritual ancestors.

May this blessing flow into every realm, level, and dimension. May these lineages heal and rise into the light, and, when the time is right, may we reconnect with one another in light and love. May this small book open our eyes and bless and enrich us on many levels and in many dimensions. I honor you, Aumakua, ancestors and spiritual forebears who came before us and made my path straight, and I dedicate this book to you.

Acknowledgements by Shantidevi

I thank you, those ancestors who came before me, for the gifts of life and love.

There would be no me without you, and from the bottom of my heart I honor and revere your lives as they were lived. I thank you sincerely for permitting me as your descendant, through your very existence, to learn so much of the mystery of life, the distortions of love, and the blessing of redemption through love.

In particular, I would like to thank the ancestors from my paternal grandmother's lineage, who were priests. You have long been a source of comfort and blessing, of light, and of support.

I thank you, my spiritual ancestors and teachers on my path, who through training and initiation have led me to a deeper understanding of the spiritual path we follow as human beings.

I thank my soul for all the many valuable and insightful memories from the past; these are the parts that make up my potential as a whole, slowly reassembling themselves, bit by bit, piece by piece.

I now feel deeply connected with Heaven and Earth, with the angels and the Ascended Masters. I feel nourished and blessed by your spiritual lineages.

I have been granted permission to learn that unfulfilled love in family systems ultimately sends us on a quest for the one true lasting love.

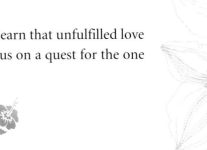

That I am currently following this path of memory, as are so many other people, is a great gift, particularly since we have been lacking love for so long and in such pain.

And so we grow in understanding of our true selves. May everything that heals within us be a source of light, inspiration, and a blessing for everyone on this incredibly beautiful planet who takes this path home with and after us.

May we all remember who we really are.

Remember:
You are light from light
Love from love…

Introduction by Jeanne Ruland

What happened earlier in your life does not matter.
Your outward appearance is of no importance.
What other people say about you is irrelevant. Within your
*   innermost being, you bear the spark of God, radiant,*
*   unchanging, and pure.*
Step into the place given to you by God. Take up your
*   life in your loving hands and open yourself. Receive the*
*   blessing of Heaven and Earth. Remember. Awaken.*
Enter the hallowed halls of initiation in your heart. Your
*   higher self, your inner teacher, resides within you,*
*   waiting for you to reach out and make contact.*
You can shape your life in love, peace, and joy, and pass on
*   your light to other people.*
Everything is already within you.

AUMAKUA—the blessing and potential of our being

"You who came before us and made straight our path, we thank and bless you. We are ready to accept our potential in all its magnitude and power, awakening the true power within us and playing our part in the grand plan."

Why do we use the word Aumakua? It comes from the Hawaiian and is an "umbrella term" for the energy of the Higher Self in which the liberated powers of the wisdom of both our spiritual ancestors and our family forebears are gathered. Along with our physical forebears, our spiritual ancestors may also include animal spirits, plant beings, minerals, Nature's realms, angelic realms, the ranks of the masters, the starry skies above, traditions of healers and priests from many cultures, and more. Aumakua describes the entire potential that is within us, inside the very cells in our body, an awakening through which we are united with our souls. The term Aumakua is more exhaustive and extensive than others used to describe ancestors and heirs. This book addresses our ancestral lineage, our true and divine heritage, and the potential within us, on a human, spiritual, and mental level. When we recognize who we are and where we come from, we will finally understand why we are here.

We have reached the end of a 16.4 billion year creation cycle. Creation is nearing completion. We are midway in waking from our "Sleeping Beauty" slumbers, in sitting up and thinking about what we really are.

As souls we have lived through and experienced a great deal during this cycle, each of us in our unique way. It is time for us to reconnect with the Source, to heal the old cycles, and to take a new direction in harmony with Creation.

When the circles are reconnected and unbroken, a new era of peace will dawn.

The circles that connect us include those of our ancestors and relatives who play such an important part in shaping our childhood, and through whom we adopt certain models or patterns of behavior.

The slings and arrows of fortune can create gaps or fractures in the circles, as can fear, betrayal, anger, discord, dramas caused by the misuse of sacred energy. They can be the consequences of a cry for justice, becoming embroiled in disputes, strife, sickness, or addiction, lasting generations as old sufferings are constantly rekindled. We can carry on as before and pass on the old patterns of behavior, or if we are ready to acknowledge our creative potential and orient ourselves more toward our spiritual nature, we can begin to steer an entirely new course and achieve a wholly new perspective on these circles.

We play a major role in shaping this creation, and it represents our greatest chance of choosing new paths and weaving new patterns in harmony with the divine matrix for our children and their children. We too will one day join the ranks of our ancestors and keep watch over our descendants.

I am delighted to be writing this small book with Shantidevi.

We approach the topic from different angles and so can shed light on various aspects and broaden our perspectives on our ancestors, on working toward liberation, and on our potential. Shantidevi and I have long been following a shared path and enjoy both a very fruitful exchange of ideas and many wonderful experiences. In the seminars we have jointly led, we have released many old blockages and activated so much potential. The idea to combine trauma/shadow and potential work has simply been a stroke of genius, as it is our potential that helps us to call to our conscious minds the shadows, challenges, and obstacles within us, and in so doing to liberate ourselves.

It is our aim with this book and the practical and easy exercises it includes to help you along your path, using the insights we have gained from several years of practical work. We hope it will be a blessing for many.

As the Dalai Lama once said, it is not intelligent to be unhappy.

In order to usher in a new era of peace, joy, and freedom, we must realize that the time has now come to awaken these qualities in our lives and to bid farewell to old patterns, close circles, gain insights, accept our true legacy, and release our true potential.

We are the capstone of an epoch and the dawn of a new age. Each of us has within us all we need to take control of our lives with strength and power; when we recognize and expose that potential, we shall be able to master any challenge.

May this book bring you, the reader, many insights and intuitions, open new paths, and reveal the many layers of this work while leading you toward a higher dimension and a wider perspective. Putting this new knowledge into practice will become easier with the book's exercises, rituals, and meditations, allowing you to activate the potential that lives within you.

We wish you much joy and great insight as you read on. Blessed be the divine in you, in me, and in each and every one of us.

Aloha nui loa
Jeanne

Introduction by Shantidevi

Immerse yourself in love…
Surrender pain to grace,
To the redeeming heart of God…
Rise again and shine…

Our ancestors are our origins, our power, and our heritage. The themes that concern them mirror our own spiritual path and potential but often also the obstacles and stumbling blocks we face. We often hesitate to connect with them fully because we are scared of what remains unresolved and of the burdens we have unconsciously helped to bear. It is only when we turn to them in love once again that we will open ourselves up to their blessings and the full potential that lies within our ancestral lineage. It is just waiting to be brought to the world as a great gift.

We are never apart from love. Love permeates us and is our deepest essence, the power of the highest manifestation and the most powerful healing force in the universe. More and more people are awakening to their true selves, even if old identities continue to shroud our light like dark veils from time to time. But beneath such veils, we are luminous, magnificent light-beings just waiting to gift radiance to the world. We are safe, secure, invulnerable, and immortal in our true beings and the more people that rediscover their home in love, the easier it will be for global change to occur.

For many people "ancestor work" conjures up images of some grave destiny, recurrent patterns that are unconsciously passed down from generation to generation, suffering, and pain. We have become too accustomed to focusing on the things that are not good or that we would wish to be different, instead of heeding what has been there all along. Our physical and our spiritual ancestors have hidden treasures for us, about whose existence we often have little idea. We have accumulated an infinite variety of experiences and have developed abilities through lifetimes along our spiritual paths that often remain concealed beneath old vows and promises. However, they are there ready and waiting to be set free from dusty treasure chests.

Exactly the same thing is true of the potential within our genetic ancestral lineage, our family. We are always incarnated in a family that will best serve our development. This can often also involve activating old wounds in order for them to heal and setting off in search of true love and our true selves. We will discover many different aspects of ourselves on that journey, and it is during this extremely special time that we are allowed to take these aspects and shape them into the precious being that we truly are. When we learn to pay attention to the good aspects, we feel strengthened. The time has come to refocus on our potential and establish a positive heritage within ourselves, so that it may flourish, mature, and ripen. We need a world in which we can follow new paths.

As Marianne Williamson once said, it is our light, not our darkness, that most frightens us. Our deepest shadows (things that are forgotten and suppressed) are our own inner light, our own divine consciousness. We would like to show you paths of transformation, reminding you of your own light and the light of your Aumakua, inspiring you to let go of the past and enter a new era with joy and ease. We want to encourage you to trust yourself so that your true being can bless your life and everything you touch.

It has been a great joy to write this small book with my spiritual sister, Jeanne. In our joint seminars, I have always found that we complement each other so well and that what motivates our work comes from the same spiritual space. We combine work to bring liberation from past issues with work to free up potential, and provide the practical tips and suggestions from our toolkit and treasure chests that will provide support for you on your path to a fulfilled life.

Namaste—the divine within me greets the divine within you.
Shantidevi

Preserving ancient knowledge

There was a time when the Old Ones were revered in every culture, and the places where our ancestors lived were visited by those seeking advice, consolation, support, and inspiration. The true potential and spiritual abilities acquired would often be passed down from one generation to the next; the knowledge was preserved and a new generation could live according to its precepts. Today, we still encounter many ancient traditions and ceremonies that date back to the dawn of time and are still being passed down, including, for example, sweat lodges, age-old healing traditions, and much more.

In myths and fairy tales we also find accounts of a hero or heroine gaining inspiration and strength from the realms of their ancestors. Cinderella is one of the best-known fairy tales, in which the heroine draws great support at the graveside of her mother and goes on to find her fortune despite all the challenges she faces.

At this point I would like to describe my own insights into the Aumakua, our ancestors. As part of my shamanic training I once journeyed into many different cells in my body (stem cells, heart cells, brain cells, bone cells) in order to experience their energy. The bone cells surprised me the most. Although all else had long since passed away and dissolved, as a bone cell I could quite happily sit in the earth for eons and remember everything that had once been. I preserved this knowledge with great patience.

Our bones consist of different minerals and crystalline structures that are capable of storing considerable amounts of knowledge. They store everything we have learned, experienced, and undergone emotionally during our lifetimes. This knowledge is preserved via bone, stone, and crystalline structures, not to mention the Earth's network of crystal lattices. When the time comes, it can be recalled and transformed.

If we assume that there is an eternal spark shining within us ("I am, I was, I shall be"), then great ancient knowledge from the essence of our souls is stored in stone, mineral, and bone and can be recalled. The ancient places of our ancestors, stone circles, gravesites, and religious buildings may draw us to them; the spiritual aspects of bones may call out to us, so that we can remember, awaken, and free ourselves once more, and recognize who we really are. I have traveled to many places and have seen and experienced many things in my life to date. Some of the places I visited changed and transformed me forever, some entranced me, and in others my tears flowed and I felt terrible pain until I remembered with courage. Something within me was liberated, awakened with a kiss, deeply moved, until the end of time.

How many old bones, stones, skull oracles, and ancestor oracles are there on this planet?

What is so special about the ancient places of this Earth, about crystal skulls? What is stored in the eternal ice, in water crystals, to be released again when the ice melts? Our souls remember so that the seeds long since planted within us can germinate. Our essence lies stored in much more than we can imagine.

Naturally this includes things that are extremely uplifting but also events stored in human history, including gruesome murders, rituals, and wars. It also includes memories and the expansive, eternal potential that is linked to the stars and to the entire universe. Contact with this potential may bring the deepest pain yet also the greatest freedom.

We live in a time of grace in which we are increasingly rising above the material world, and in which our spiritual, divine potential is being awakened. We are reaching new dimensions and can now see further, deeper, and in greater detail. Some things can be transformed simply by being seen with new eyes.

Our Aumakua, who are enlightened in eternity through recognition of the divine essence within themselves, send eternal blessings and wait silently for us to complete our journeys here.

They want to initiate us into our true legacy, which is not of this world. We would like to take you with us on this exciting journey and perhaps reawaken something within you. We are entering a new era together, and within each of us lies huge potential, unique strength, and infinite capabilities. There are no boundaries; anything is possible. If we believe the impossible is possible, then it can become so. Your genetic and spiritual ancestors await you, and have done so for eons. If you discover your true potential, no lives in your ancestral lineage will have been led in vain; we are liberating more than we can possibly imagine.

Our ancestors as a mirror of timeless patterns of the soul

I am extremely grateful that Jeanne and I are able to approach this topic from different perspectives. Jeanne provides a huge wealth of experience from shamanism, and from Hawaiian Huna in particular, and from numerous initiations. Her clairvoyance has been a great blessing for many. We both work intensively with transformation and liberation and take great joy in helping people to achieve their fullest potential.

I have been practicing reincarnation therapy since the early 1990s and it always shows me that current problems are expressions of timeless patterns of the soul. We progress from unconsciousness to ever greater conscious levels. I see our spiritual ancestors as being profoundly linked to our spiritual paths, our experiences in times gone by, and our former

lives. It is here that we experienced light and shade and forgot who we really are; we played all sorts of roles in order to combine them and in the end shape our own potential.

Now it is time for this potential to create a precious jewel. There have never been so many therapies and seminars available for personal growth, and it is a great privilege for me to investigate those experiences that enabled us to achieve our full potential. Experiences in which we can sense how it feels to be connected with our divine potential, and in which we can express our light consciousness here on Earth in our own unique way. Such memories function as beacons on our spiritual journey. We are not drawn to places and cultures by chance; our soul knows them. I have experienced this repeatedly in places such as Glastonbury, Stonehenge, the Egyptian temples, in Córdoba or Hawaii, places where I simply feel that I am coming home. We are spiritually anchored to such places, and when we set foot there again, a great gateway opens up in our souls and we connect with the ancient light traditions to which we belong.

In the same way, our genetic ancestral lineage cannot be separated from our spiritual paths and we find the behavioral patterns that belong to us among the ranks of our ancestors, the advice we need to achieve our highest potential, and the support and encouragement that goes with it. However, we can also discover issues that lurk in the shadows, that remain unresolved. I regularly meet people who are like light-bringers for their ancestors; they touch upon unresolved issues with their love and compassion, they honor and respect the ways of their ancestors, and they bring liberation for many souls from our ancestral lineage who have not yet managed to go into the light.

Since the end of the 1990s, I have incorporated spiritual aspects into systemic family therapy in my seminars, working with the aid of the spiritual world and with healing circles. In my experience love is like a stream of grace, flowing into issues awaiting healing and setting them free. Through our unconscious love, we have been loyal to the pain, irreconcilability, and unresolved aspects of our ancestors; the time has come to see their potential and to declare our commitment to the fulfillment of our ancestors' dreams, to continue what they may have been unable to complete. In this way we can take possession of the abundance yet to be lived out and pass it on to our children in love.

Our lineage also includes our light-filled ancestors, those that have long since gone into the light and now look down on their descendants with the deepest love as they give their blessings. Making a connection with our spiritual ancestors and the spiritual world opens up a new and more straightforward dimension to healing work, from which endless blessings flow.

LIFE and DEATH from a Hawaiian perspective

There is a light behind everything, an eternal current of life at work. Life comes, life goes, and life returns, as we are eternal. The Hawaiian word for the flux of life is "Ola." Hidden in the depths of the word is the eternally pulsing, vibrating light. For the Kahunas, the guardians of the secret, light is a symbol of energy and consciousness without limits. The expression

"Wai Ola" is found in many of Hawaii's legends, stories, and prayers. It means the "water of life" or the "flow of life." Life is a constant stream that does not end even in death, which is a continuation of life but in another direction, dimension, and state. Death is not the opposite of life, but instead a part of it.

The Hawaiians consider death to be a part of life, as belonging to life's ongoing, eternal processes. It is as commonplace as the natural circle of life, the transformation we witness in Nature when a bird emerges from an egg, a caterpillar transforms into a butterfly, and a seed becomes a tree. Each of us has a task in life to fulfill. Our higher selves ensure that we develop this understanding of life; it is left to us whether we do so in a matter of hours or two hundred years, and with joy or reluctance. There are many levels beyond the one that is visible. There is no timeline in our culture, only waves, circles, and cycles. Time can stretch forever and so it is not important when an event takes place. "Everything is good the way it is" is a very important concept on Hawaii: it provides deep trust in the power that permeates all things, creates everything, and takes it all back once again. Death is seen as an inner space in which individuals look back on the life they have led and revive old friendships, a space in which the vital powers refresh and renew, and in which we prepare for new experiences of growth.

Each night in our dreams, we leave our body in order to go into this "interior world space." We can also access it through meditation or trance, and on shamanistic journeys. We were born out of this spiritual realm and are in regular contact with it. We will return there, perhaps to be born out of it again. Our Higher Self dwells in this eternal space, where everything is possible. It is from this realm that the waves of energy that can engulf us and carry us off into wholly new experiences and levels of consciousness emanate. It is from here that the souls we receive on a wave of energy during the act of conception come. We can enter this inner space at any point, and indeed do so when we go to sleep in order to make contact with the wisdom of our souls, to allow past events to rise to the surface, to examine and change them. It is here that we can meet our ancestors and experience profound initiations into our true being.

The teaching of the eternal nature of our souls is found in many cultures around the world, including in our own ancient roots.

OUR GENETIC
ANCESTORS

Seeing our parents in a new light

Our parents and our relatives are among our most important teachers; they help shape our view of the world, how we understand ourselves, and our relationships with ourselves and with others.

Viewed from a spiritual perspective, they reflect and reinforce the behavioral patterns we bring with us; they encourage or suppress aspects of us to which we need to pay attention. They give us the greatest gift of all—our lives.

We encounter those closest to us repeatedly, interacting with them in many different ways, sometimes challenging each other, sometimes blessing each other or acting as angels of healing. We plan it all together at a higher level and out of love.

We can often experience this in a very different way, of course. For example, I struggled for many years with the fact that my mother had a long-term illness and was often no longer able to deal well with life or to develop her full potential. The life she lived out before me was mostly one of bravery and sacrificial love, and as a result was not an ideal role model for me as an independent, healthy, powerful, dignified woman. At some point in a therapy session I realized that it was precisely through the way she was that I came to follow the medicinal and subsequently spiritual path, perhaps at first in order to help her, and of course myself, as I had been shaped by her. It was through my mother that I learned compassion and loving care. The realization that she was precisely the right person to direct me to the path that ultimately led to my vocation made me cry tears of liberation and reconciliation. In such moments, in the sense of radical forgiveness from a higher perspective, we may come to understand that nothing intrinsically "wrong" has happened, however much we may have missed out on events or experiences, or indeed suffered pain.

Parents who have endured difficult times, such as the trauma of war, illness, addiction, or adversity, are often unable to give their children what they most need to flourish and to develop their potential and natural sense of self-worth. However, we often forget that our parents have always done the best they could in the circumstances. We often have a more generous view of our parents once we become parents ourselves and experience how often we are overstretched as a father or mother.

People often spend their entire lives with *my parents (father/mother) didn't love me (enough)* metaphorically stamped on their foreheads. They repeat this narrative of having missed out to themselves again and again.

Marshall Rosenberg, the founder of nonviolent communication, said in one of his seminars that the pain we experience caused by a particular event amounts as a rule to only five percent of the pain we will carry around with us due to that event. The remaining ninety-five percent of the pain is caused by our interpretation of the event and the entrenched beliefs that arise as a result. Examples include: I am not good enough; I am not lovable; I'm not allowed to be me; I must have done something wrong, that's why they treat me like this.

It is especially difficult to find peace in particular if you keep brooding on old pain and reflecting on absent parents.

The following exercise may help you to reactivate the current of love and gratitude for your parents and make it flow again.

Exercise:
What do I love about my mother (my father)?

Spend at least seven minutes telling a person you trust what you like, appreciate, and love about your mother or father. It will be helpful if your companion repeats: "What do you love about your mother?" during this exercise. They should not pass any comment on your list of points, however.

Write down the points that you think of, looking at your childhood, your teenage years, and your adulthood.

Here are a few examples.

What I love about my mother:

- That she often sang to me.
- That she was so good at baking.
- That she took me to church when I was very young and that I got to hear that uplifting, beautiful organ music at such an early age.
- The memory of the warm, safe feeling when I crept into her bed after a bad dream and fell asleep in her arms.
- That she has such a big heart.
- That she is so creative.
- That she likes to cook my favorite food when I come to visit.
- That she likes to laugh and have fun.
- That we can enjoy a spa day together.
- …

Then ask yourself what you are grateful to your mother for.

I am grateful:

- That she always sewed us beautiful things.
- That she always magically put a lovely meal on the table, even when she was sick and felt unwell.
- That she so patiently taught me to crochet and knit.
- That she always listened to my problems when I was small.
- That she often helped me to do my homework.
- That I was/am able to talk to her so easily.
- That I have inherited much of her beauty (her eyes, her hair, etc.)
- That I learned to love from her.
- …

I always find it helpful to swap roles at this point. Ask your exercise partner why they love their mother and are grateful to her. They may mention things you have experienced yourself, as is often the case with the law of resonance, and you will be reminded of other beautiful and positive things about your mother (father).

I have carried out the following meditation on "finding peace with your parents" in my family constellation seminars for many years and have seen how people's views of their parents suddenly change. Many of those taking part have wept tears of relief as they finally realized just how much love was there. They learned how to recognize the good in their parents and to remember that love was present at the beginning, however complicated the relationship became later.

Take your time over this journey and you will connect with the Archangel Haniel. He will support you in taking on your true greatness and in seeing your parents in all their uniqueness. He will give you the gift of seeing with God's eyes, in truth and clarity.

If another light-filled companion should appear on this journey, however, trust your inner perception and "go with the flow."

Meditation:
Finding peace with your parents

Make yourself comfortable. Close your eyes.

Take a few deep breaths. Let go of tension on each outbreath and allow yourself to be completely present in the room.

Feel the ground beneath you and your connection to the Earth. Allow yourself to feel the love of the Earth surrounding and spreading through you with its vital force, and providing you with everything you need right now.

Connect with the heart of God, with the source of all being; allow divine love to surround and fill you from above, in love and protection, anchoring you in love from Heaven and Earth.

Now call the Archangel Haniel to your side, the angel of clarity and truth who helps us see the world through God's eyes. Allow Haniel and the angels of healing who have now gathered here to lay their hands on your body and to flood you with golden light, letting the healing and love required for this inner journey flow into you.

Your vibration will increase, and Haniel will help you see things in a new light, as if seeing through God's eyes, without being influenced by the stories, ideas, and memories that you carry within yourself.

Haniel is now touching your Third Eye and gifting you the memory of your soul, allowing you to see your parents lying in an intimate embrace and the colors of their aura change in the act of love that caused your soul to incarnate with these

35

two people. You will feel that there was love and ecstasy at that time and that the dance of your parents' energies was the invitation your soul accepted and through which you said yes to them. Haniel is now helping you to recognize, from a higher perspective, why they were the perfect parents for you, despite any difficulties you may have encountered later, and why these challenges were important for your development. You can see the riches that have come into being through this intimacy.

Now let go of it again.

Once again Haniel touches your Third Eye and gifts you an image of your mother as a young woman, and you see her with her dreams and desires; you are looking deep into her heart as if through the eyes of God. You can see what lit a spark inside her heart and what was really important to her.

And now in your mind's eye you see the central theme in your mother's life playing out before you. You see her potential, the positive legacy you inherited from her, regardless of whether she was able to live this potential completely in beauty, or only partially or in a distorted way. Or perhaps she has forgotten it completely. You both see and sense this positive legacy.

And Haniel now touches your Third Eye and your heart, gifting you a memory of the very special moment when your mother first held you in her arms after you were born, and when you met, soul to soul, looking deep into one another's eyes, as she realized the miracle to which she had just given birth.

Now allow yourself to accept completely the gift of life from your mother. Then this image recedes again.

And Haniel touches your Third Eye once again and gifts you the image of your father as a young man. You see him with his dreams and desires; you are looking deep into his heart as if through the eyes of God. You can see what lit a spark inside his heart and what was really important to him.

And now in your mind's eye you see the central theme in your father's life. You see his potential, regardless of whether he was able to live this out in beauty, or only partially or in a distorted way. Perhaps he has forgotten it completely. You both see and sense this positive legacy.

And Haniel once again touches your Third Eye and your heart, gifting you a memory of the very special moment when your father first held you in his arms after you were born, and when you met, soul to soul, looking deep into one another's eyes as he realized what a miracle he had conceived and that it came about through his love of your mother.

Accept the gift of life from him completely too. Then let it go again …

And Haniel touches your Third Eye once more, and you look at yourself and see yourself as God sees you. You recognize how the central themes running through the lives of your mother and father intertwine in you, creating something entirely new and uniquely valuable that is you.

And now a path of light unfolds before you. A shining symbol that represents the highest potential of your soul appears before you. Haniel now helps you to understand what this symbol means. Feel and experience how this light symbol moves toward you to become one with you in your own way in your own time.

Allow the benevolent power of your highest potential to permeate you, taking up ever more space inside you with each breath in a way that feels exactly right for you.

Feel once again the blessing of your parents upon you and your path, the blessing of their souls that you may become as God intended, independent of their personal expectations and wishes.

And now this blessing flows like a shower of sparkling light from Heaven and Earth into you, allowing you to be yourself entirely and so that what you have to offer can make the world a more beautiful place.

Open your heart as you would open a door and allow the power of this light symbol, representing your highest potential, to shine out into the world. Touch every person who is important to you with this light, in the full knowledge that you are sharing the beauty of your heart with those you love and with all of Creation.

Now bring yourself very gently back into the room where your body is resting. Start to breathe in and out a little more deeply to return to yourself fully. The moment you open your eyes, you are awake and refreshed.

The role of the family

All the issues that are relevant to us—both in light and shadow, good and bad—can be found within the family. Khalil Gibran was quite right when he likened the role of fathers and mothers to a strong bow used by the Creator to fire his beloved arrows into the world. In terms of our special potential, the things that bring us joy and make our hearts sing are often indicators of our special talents, many of which are encouraged in our families and are a natural part of us.

There are of course patterns in families that still require healing, both within us personally and within the family group, along with issues from which we can grow and learn. If we want to develop abilities (that up to then it had not been possible to do), our soul often creates situations in which we experience exactly the opposite of what we want to learn; for example, we experience weakness when we want to develop strength.

Pain leads us to the path of change. We experience conflict and struggle when seeking peace in order to fully appreciate peace when it comes. We experience judgment, shame, and perhaps even humiliation, when seeking to rediscover our dignity and self-worth.

Many years ago, during a meditation I realized that the unfulfilled potential of our ancestors was like a source—a reservoir—of pent-up energy; at some stage it will be filled to the brim and a fresh breeze will cause a wave to break over the edge and spill out, bringing fertility and vitality to a new

piece of land. We are the ones who bring completion to what was unfinished. We are living in a time of great grace and no longer have to struggle to survive like many of our ancestors. We have the time and leisure to focus on personal growth, to seek and find new paths, which is how we heal ourselves and our family. *All that heals within us has a healing effect on collective humanity, and all that heals in the greater whole has a direct effect upon us as individuals.*

Our names are also important. Like life itself, they are a gift from our parents. *Nomen est omen* (the name is a sign). The meaning of our names may give us hints about our being and what we have to learn through experience.

Certain family names have been passed down through the generations. In some families there is a whole sequence of Marys or Henrys, for example. This may indicate a deep connection with the legacy of our eponymous ancestors, with their talents and gifts, but equally, also with their unresolved, overshadowed issues. Those who bear names that are passed down through the family often deliver freedom to the forebears who share that name.

The resurfacing of supressed emotions

We all know that we are aware of certain things, including issues we appreciate and love, those with which we have made our peace, or those that we faced, no matter how difficult it was to do so but that have turned out well in the end. However, there is also a shadow side within us, including the things we deny, push away, and repress because they are simply too much or because we do not want to admit them to ourselves. These unwanted issues do not simply disappear, annoyingly enough, but instead have a habit of returning. If we have an unhealed emotional wound, such as having been left by someone we loved, we continue to attract into our lives the very kind of people who leave us, reopening this old wound. This causes pain, but it also offers a chance for healing.

Like a mirror held up to the outside world, life reveals the things we repress and do not like. They resurface in certain situations, sometimes unpleasant, acting as reminders. We have long fought against, judged, and denied these shadows in the outside world, unable to see the opportunity they present for healing. It is time to take back the repressed part of ourselves projected onto the outside world, take it into our hearts, and feel it there.

In the same way that we repress the things we do not like in our personal lives, there are also patterns of repression in families: the collective unconscious. This is where events that are painful to experience, suffer, grieve for, and process are stored. During the two world wars of the 20th century, for example, many families were touched by dreadful suffering, experiencing the horrors of warfare, fear of death, separation, the loss of loved ones, displacement, flight, rape, and the emotional paralysis that arises from living through ongoing traumatic events.

The repressed collective memory of the family contains troubles and burdens passed on from generation to generation, including unresolved pain grieving for relatives who died prematurely, unborn children, miscarriages, abortions, and stillbirths.

When a mother loses a child, for example, and is unable to mourn the loss sufficiently, a part of her becomes frozen inside, and she can no longer give her living children and her husband enough love. This is deeply tragic.

I see it repeatedly in systematic family work. And too often it reveals how entire generations can be deeply traumatized, their emotions frozen by conflict and the flow of love interrupted. The focus switches to surviving and rebuilding after the destruction caused by a traumatic event, and feelings fall by the wayside.

The positive news, however, is that forgotten potential and talents can resurface, even after remaining repressed and unresolved for generations. A child who is very gifted musically may suddenly appear in an "unmusical" family, and long-buried scientific or creative abilities have a habit of resurfacing too.

Family secrets: The consequences of failing to honor family members

Repressed issues tend to resurface, either mirroring something in the outside world (issues reintroduced into families by outside influences) or as something that is unconsciously repeated in subsequent generations. In order for healing to take place, past issues and events must resurface, be witnessed and felt, or a connection to the past established so that peace can prevail.

An all too common example is the suppressed rage of parents after separation. A child will often pick up on emotions that both adults are unwilling to feel and will act them out. It is a clear indicator of family conflict, and one that cannot simply be ignored. However, if the parents work through their issues, the situation with their child can often become relaxed once more.

Suppressed parental issues manifest themselves not only with their children, however; they can often have an effect across a number of generations. People whose forebears have been driven out of their homeland often find it difficult to find their place in life. Something within them still roams like a refugee. In many families, the dead from the last two world wars who were not properly mourned still exert an influence. An entire generation was in a state of shock, as it were, and people were unable to grieve fully.

One of the things that hurts us most deeply is when we feel we are not seen, honored, and respected for who we are with all that we have experienced. And so "being noticed" is a gift we can give to our ancestors to bring deep healing and allow them to find peace; it is a question of recognizing in love what was and what is.

I would like to give you a clear example of how repressed issues in a family can resurface over generations. In around 1900, an illegitimate baby girl was born into a family, and at the time this was considered a scandal, so the family rejected her at birth and gave her up for adoption. This secret was known only to the men of the family and was seen as a youthful indiscretion of one of its past members, passed on *sotto voce* from one to the next.

What is striking about this particular family tree is that only the eldest son of this particular ancestor actually had children who then went on to have children of their own; the second son remained unmarried and the third had three children, of whom none had offspring of their own. Two of the ancestor's descendants brought up the children their wives had brought into the marriage, however. The side branch of the family descending from this ancestor's brother featured a nephew who adopted a child from outside the family and a niece who helped to bring up a child who was not her own. Children in this family group were repeatedly brought into its circle because a child had once been excluded. The issue of adoption even resurfaced two generations later. The descendants were unconsciously atoning for a guilt incurred and repressed by the giving up of a child in 1900.

Healing circles for your ancestors

Healing circles are a great opportunity to restore peace and heal old wounds in family systems.

To conduct a healing circle, gather together a few like-minded people (healing circles that include family members are particularly good) who are clearly focused on divine love, prepared to honor and respect events from the past, and who are prepared to identify and address in love issues that await healing. We sometimes feel the repressed emotions of our ancestors, but it is important for our consciousness to be wholly present in the here and now, in our hearts, and to avoid becoming tangled up with our feelings. We are loving witnesses to the burdensome fate of our ancestors. Hence it is good to stand in a circle and hold hands while maintaining a clear focus. Choosing a ritual leader is also recommended, someone who will name and guide the energies that arise.

During the ritual, it is important *to concentrate only on what is ready to be healed at this time and for which you have the strength.*

Depending on the people involved, I have often seen how powerful prayers, mantras, and sacred songs can be, including *dona nobis pacem* (grant us peace), *Kyrie, eleison* (Lord, have mercy), or the Guru Rinpoche mantra *Om Ah Hung Benza Guru Pema Siddhi Hung* (Blessings of the Diamond Master born from lotus)—the most powerful cleansing mantra in Tibetan Buddhism according to the Dalai Lama.

Many of our ancestors who were unable to find peace did not go into the light upon death but remained earthbound. For this reason, at the end of a healing circle, we invite all our deceased forebears (and only those) whose wish and destiny it is to now go into the light, to take the journey back into great love and return home with the angels. We deliver all the others into the hands of God and the loving arms of healing angels.

Procedure for the circle

Play some pleasant background music. Stand in a circle and hold hands.

Center your concentration on your hearts.

Make a connection with the heart of the Earth below you, breathing in the power of the Earth so that you are wholly grounded in the here and now.

Make a connection with the heart of God above you and feel how the light of love surrounds you completely. Feel how you are now clearly focused on the love of Heaven and Earth. Call upon your guardian angel and spiritual leaders to stand behind you, so they can reinforce your light channel and you can become a clear expression for love and empathy.

Call the radiance of grace, divine mercy, the power of Christ (or whatever name you give to divine love), the angels of healing, and all your light-filled ancestors to you, asking them all for their support in healing an old wound in your family system. Now mention an issue that is currently weighing on your mind (for example, unresolved grief over a grandmother's brother who died in the war, or an ancestor's children that were lost, unborn, or died prematurely).

Let your love and empathy flow (you might find that you shed a few tears). If your ancestors were religious, it can help to say a prayer (for example, the Lord's Prayer, a Hail Mary, or The Lord is My Shepherd). If it feels right, hum or sing until you feel peace. Honor and acknowledge the destiny of your ancestors just as it was.

Bow before the greatness of their souls with the greeting *namaste* and tell them: "*The divine within us sees and greets the divine within you, that which cannot be damaged or destroyed.*"

Imagine you are now delivering all your ancestors into God's hands and the arms of the angels of healing.

Let your love and empathy continue to flow until you feel at peace.

Now call the Elohim from the golden beam of light, the angels of homecoming, with a golden pillar of light, to be among you. Invite all those of your deceased ancestors who have been able to find peace through this healing circle, and whose desire and destiny is to step into the light, to look for the light-filled hands of the angels, to grasp them, and then to go home into the light. Ask them to take all their energy with them and to leave this dimension.

Lift them into the light with your love. Wish them a beautiful journey home and tell them once again *that there is love that shall remain between their souls and yours.*

Feel how the energy field dissolves and becomes ever more radiant and light-filled, until peace reigns in the room and it is once again entirely clear.

Parental blessing

There was a time when it was common for parents to bless their children upon leaving home. They did so in the knowledge that they had done their best for their children and that they trusted the "good seed" planted in their offspring. However, it is a rare occurrence today; children leave the parental home without a blessing and without the ritual acknowledgment that their parents are giving them their independence, handing on responsibility for their own lives, and looking upon them with generosity and benevolence. I see it as a very special act of grace when parents and/or grandparents bless their children and grandchildren, such as when celebrating becoming an adult or getting married, or more symbolically, in a family constellation.

Should you now feel the desire to bless your (grown-up) children, perhaps on an appropriate occasion, use one of these blessing formulations, adjusting it accordingly for your situation.

Blessing

"My dear son (daughter), as your mother (father) I bless you for your whole life. May everything I have given you in love become a source of strength and blessing within you. May you stay healthy and find success and fulfillment. May you always know that life loves you, so you can develop and achieve your highest potential and in your own unique identity. I wish with all my heart for you to have a good and happy life, full of trust in your abilities and in life. My love goes with you."

The important ritual of releasing and healing

Introduction

To carry out this special ritual it is important to choose a time and a space in which you will feel safe, secure, and undisturbed. It can be helpful to conduct the ritual in a group, so that you feel supported throughout the process and your energy can be enhanced. If there are several participants, choose someone to lead the proceedings and, if necessary, to help the others stay grounded and in the here and now. Playing gentle, calming background music can help, and you may need some handkerchiefs as well!

The aim of the ritual is to make peace with our parents and ancestors as well as with our own feelings and personal history. If you tend to react very emotionally, it is best not to conduct this ritual on your own. It is important to begin by taking yourself and your needs seriously, to feel and express your own repressed emotions. We can only heal what we also feel, but take care not to get too caught up in the emotions you experience. If we develop a deep understanding of our ancestors without having taken *ourselves* seriously first, it will result in a kind of "spiritual bypass" and *our* wounds and feelings of lack or of missing out will not heal in any depth.

It is often not only privations and grief that surface, but also rage and defiance. Rage is always a replacement emotion for unfulfilled needs, however. Should you experience rage, allow yourself to feel it for a short time and then go deeper.

Feel the pain behind it, the pain from which your rage was also protecting you, and express it. Ensure that a part of you is always present in the here and now and that you do not get lost in your feelings. It is helpful to be aware of where in your body you experience these emotions, to feel your feet on the ground, and to keep your eyes open.

One of the most profound healing experiences occurs when, in the end, everything, whether good or bad, is considered with affection, honor, and respect. This is as true for ourselves and everything we believe we must keep hidden as it is for our ancestors.

In the knowledge that each person always does and has done the best they can in their own way, we will have the opportunity to honor and acknowledge the lives of our ancestors and the often burdensome destinies they experienced.

We will give back those burdens that we bore for them out of unconscious love and call for the energies that we gave to them in return to be given back to us. We will get back our inner child, who may still be seated in front of its parents, ever hopeful of receiving the things it never had. We assume responsibility for our own healing, which creates freedom for both sides. We cease to expect from our parents something they were never destined to experience and were therefore unable to give. We prepare to seek and discover support in places where love can flow and nourish us.

Make sure you allow enough time for the various steps of the ritual to take place and allow a little extra for yourself at the end. Do not put yourself under any time pressure or schedule important tasks for the hours immediately after the ritual.

Preparation

The space

This ritual is an act of love for yourself and for your ancestors. Make sure the room is suitable for the occasion. You could decorate it with flowers or light some candles as symbols of the light that lives in each of us, and for our light-filled ancestors and helpers from the spiritual world that are always with us. Use a spray to fragrance the room (rosewater, an Aura-Soma room spray, light-being essential oils) or burn some incense.

Your place

Make sure you have a space in which you can sit comfortably or stand should you feel like it. When we release past issues, we sometimes feel the need to move around or shake out our limbs a little. Ensure you have enough room to do this.

Your parents' and ancestors' place

Prepare a space opposite you, at a certain distance, for your parents and your other ancestors. You might like to put one or two chairs there, or a photo of your parents or a symbol that connects you with them.

Your inner child

Choose a symbol to represent your inner child, who is waiting and yearning for the things that you feel you missed out on. Follow your intuition in choosing it, then put this symbol on top of or next to your parents' place.

The fire of transformation

Choose a firepot or a candle to put in the space between you and your ancestors. I find purple candles especially helpful because I always work with the violet flame of transformation of Master Saint Germain. This fire is a great gift from the spiritual world, transforming all that passes through it into pure energy, and ensuring that the burdens that we let go do not return as burdens for our parents or ancestors, but as pure, clarified energy.

Music

Choose some music. You might want to listen to something calming and solely instrumental for the ritual itself, followed by some gentle music that touches you emotionally to finish with, a piece that will resonate with you as you welcome the New and integrate the whole process into your life. Integration is especially important when you have been in contact with your feelings, so allow yourself sufficient time.

The ritual

Getting in the mood

Once you have arranged the space for the ritual, make yourself comfortable. Feel the ground that is below you and open yourself up to the holy space within you that is accessible to rituals. Remember that time and space have no meaning in a ritual and that you are connected to the healing flow and the blessings of similar rituals in times before your own.

Build a Temple of Light

Ask the spiritual world to erect a Temple of Light in your space, a shining, luminous, sparkling, and radiant structure between worlds and beyond time. Call upon all the beings from the highest of lights that are important to you for support and blessings in your endeavor (for example, the radiance of grace, divine mercy, the liberating power of love, the energy of Christ, ascended Masters, archangels, and all the angels of the healing that is now required). Invite all your light-filled, long since liberated ancestors to bless and support this healing ritual. Wait for a moment until you can feel their light-filled energy.

Call your parents and ancestors

Invite the energy of your parents and your other ancestors to enter this Temple of Light and take their places in the space you have prepared for them, with your ancestors positioned behind your parents. Invite their spiritual guides as loving support for them too. Tell your parents and ancestors that this is a ritual of healing for all, so that peace can come and love flow again.

Express your feelings

Be aware of your parents seated opposite you (and maybe your grandparents and those ancestors you knew behind them).

Allow yourself to say aloud the feelings you could never express. This is much more powerful than simply thinking about them. Take a few minutes over each of the questions that follow.

Talk to your mother directly: "Dearest mother, I often felt so lonely as a child." Name your emotions and feel them in your body. Resist the temptation to judge your painful history from a rational perspective. Allow yourself to experience your feelings. Be honest and sincere. Take your feelings and your needs seriously.

How did you *feel* with your parents as a child?
What hurt you?
What did you miss?
What did you need and what did you want?
What did you yearn for?
What are you grateful for?

Show empathy for your parents and ancestors, honoring their destiny
Once you have shown yourself empathy, allow yourself to extend it to your parents and ancestors too. Remember that your family may have experienced some difficult twists and turns of fate, freezing their emotions so that they could only just function and making it hard for them to demonstrate and express their love. Open your heart to the problems and trials they had to face.

If you feel able, bow before them and their destiny, and honor their lives just as they were.

**Let go of the things you took upon yourself that
are no longer of use**

In this part of the ritual, many people find it helpful to stand
up. I always encourage people to let the body move or shake.
It is a process of letting go, not of relaxing. Ask the spiritual
world to support you in this transformation. Using the fire
of transformation, the next stage involves giving back everything you have taken upon yourself and which no longer
belongs to you. Gaze into the violet flames flickering between
you and your parents and ancestors. Remember that everything that goes through this fire is purified and healed and
emerges on the other side as pure energy.

Say out loud:

*"I am letting go of everything that I have consciously or
unconsciously taken upon myself from you, and I am
placing it in the violet fire of transformation so that it
may come back to you as pure energy and so that you can
be completely restored again. And I am doing this across
time and space, through all dimensions and in all incarnations."*

Take deep and gentle breaths and allow the letting go to take
place. Name the things that you know you helped to bear or
took on: feelings, burdens, patterns, and beliefs. Say them out
loud. If you are conducting the ritual in a group, what others
say will often help you name and release similar patterns. It
often helps to imagine pushing the energy you have taken on
into the fire. For example:

"I am letting go of your deep grief, which I helped carry, mom. I am letting go of the male contempt that has exerted its influence for generations. I am letting go of the belief that men are more valuable than women."

Give back all the projected thoughts and images that you took on board and adopted as beliefs. For example: Nothing will ever become of you. You aren't good enough. Your sister is just more intelligent than you. Women must serve men.

Give back responsibility

Now return the responsibilities you may have assumed and borne for your parents or ancestors. Send them out through the violet flame back to where they belong, so your ancestors can be whole again and regain their own strength.

Take back the hurt and needy child

If you sense or suspect that part of you still wants to receive from your parents the things you missed out on in life, approach your parents and ancestors. Say to them once again that you recognize that they did their very best and that you are taking back your needy child. Tell them:

"Dear parents, I now take on responsibility for healing my old wounds."

Take the symbol for your inner child and return to your place. You might also speak to your inner child. Tell it that you are taking it back and you will do everything to heal its old wounds. Tell your inner child that it can heal and grow in your heart, the place of love, and that it is infinitely precious and unique, whatever your parents may have said. Let your heart find the right words; you know best what this small person needs to hear because you came from them.

Summon your energies to return and take responsibility for yourself
Now summon your energies to return to you:

> *"I recall all the energy that I may have passed on to you from my soul energy—either consciously or unconsciously, and for whatever reason—back to me through the purifying fire of transformation, and I do this through space and time, through every dimension and incarnation. In particular, I recall all the talents and characteristics that I have given up through misunderstood love, and I take back responsibility for my own life, and I accept it."*

Gently breathe in your energy and vital power once more and let it spread through your body as you breathe out. Enjoy how it feels in your body when you once again become whole and complete.

Ask your guardian angel and your spirit guides to support this process and to help connect you with every aspect and quality of your soul again: love, self-love, self-confidence, confidence in life, strength, ease, joy, self-determination, the right and ability to set boundaries, to feel your own needs, and to stand up for them.

To conclude, say to your parents and ancestors:

"I set you free, and I set myself completely free from the burdens of the past."

Put an end to your loyalty to suffering
Remember that parents always want the best for their children (unless they become totally caught up in life's events), and yet out of loyalty we spend a long time connected to the difficult and unresolved fate of our ancestors. Now allow yourself to end your loyalty to their suffering.

Express your yearning for dignity, self-determination, and fulfillment. Tell your ancestors what you wish for and what you would like to do differently in your life. Use your feelings to touch the suppressed yearning for the highest fulfillment in your parents and ancestors.

Say out loud:

"Dear parents, dear ancestors, I am now ending my loyalty to your suffering and to repeating things that were difficult for us and I connect in deepest loyalty to your yearning for your worth, your dignity, your self-determination, and a fulfilled life. The things that, by being true to my heart, I am doing differently today, I am also doing for all my descendants and relatives."

Ask the spiritual world for healing for your ancestors, letting your love flow
Now ask an angel of healing and grace to visit each of your ancestors still in need of healing, both the living and the

dead. See how they are enfolded in the divine light of unconditional healing love and their unhealed wounds are tended
to. Ask your light-filled ancestors to help this process with
their love. Let your love and empathy flow and, if you so
wish, accompany the process with a prayer for healing for
your ancestors.

Share your riches

If it feels right, share with your ancestors the treasures you
have discovered on the path to healing and attaining consciousness. Imagine them as a source of light within you,
radiating out to your ancestors so they can remember it too.
Say to them:

> *"I would not be here without you. Thank you for the gift
> of life. I now share with you the riches that I have found
> along my path and which are part of our common heritage.
> They were never lost, only forgotten and hidden."*

Take gentle breaths and let your love flow.

Blessing

Ask your parents and ancestors for their blessing for you and your life. Feel how you receive
this blessing and send your own blessing back
through the ranks of your ancestors. Ask the
angels to go wherever the blessing does not yet
flow so that healing can flood there. Then let
go, so you can become ever more fully the person God created from his imagination.

Pass on blessings to your children and the next generation
Give your blessing with all your love to your children and grandchildren, and to all those in your family who will come after you.

Place your parents and ancestors in God's hands
Consciously place your parents and ancestors in God's hands, the best place for all those who need healing, both the living and the dead. This represents a very important step for those who took on responsibility for adults when young children and can relieve that particular burden greatly. You are free to ask your light-filled ancestors who have long since been redeemed to help with healing the family.

Accompany the dead into the light
Bow your head once more and give the *namaste* greeting before the greatness of the souls of your ancestors. Say to them:

> *"The divine within me sees and greets the divine within you, that which is invulnerable and indestructible."*

Continue to allow your love and your empathy to flow until you feel peace in the room.

Now call the Elohim from the golden beam of light, the angels of homecoming, with a golden pillar of light to your ancestors. Invite all those of your deceased ancestors who have found peace through this ritual and whose desire and destiny it is to now step into the light, to look for the light-filled hands of the angels, to grasp them, and then to go home into the light. Ask them to take all their energy with them and to leave this dimension.

Ask your light-filled ancestors for support in bringing them home in great love, and feel how the energy field dissolves and becomes ever more radiant and light-filled, until peace reigns in the room and it is once again entirely clear.

Ask the energy of the living to return
Ask the energy of your still-living ancestors whom you called or who felt called to this ritual to return to where their life is currently being lived. Thank them for being there.

Thank the spiritual world
Thank in your own way all the light-filled helpers who have supported you, and ask the Temple of Light that you built at the start of the ritual to return to the higher dimensions.

Move to the music—integration
After the ritual, move around to some gentle music for five or ten minutes, if it feels good to you, and see what else you might need to do to integrate these new things into your life.

After the ritual
Do not plan to do anything immediately after the ritual, keep the time free to do whatever you feel you need to. You might like to lie down and rest, go for a walk, take a purifying salt shower or a salt/alkaline bath. This will cleanse your aura and help you to integrate the new things into your life. When we let go of so much of our old selves, our energy

fields often need one to three days to stabilize in their new circumstances. Be gentle with yourself and respect your needs, making sure you have enough rest and sleep. It is also important to drink a lot of water or tea after the ritual to help remove toxins. Let the ritual do its work without over-analyzing or discussing it endlessly.

Your unique being

"Every human being is unique—there will never be another like any of us. We are all the bearers of untold treasures, talents, abilities, and energies. You have something unique to offer that you alone possess—be ever more aware of this."

Accept your life

Be aware that you have something to offer that belongs to you and you alone, something only you possess. You are unique and have every right to live your life, to take it in your loving hands, and shape it with joy and contentment, whatever may have happened in your childhood.

You are responsible for your life and how you live it.

You may find it useful to read "On Children", a well-known poem by Kahlil Gibran (1883–1931), which you can find in his book *The Prophet*. Recite the poem aloud a few times, speaking in the first person from the perspective of yourself as a child, for example, and feel the energetic effects. You will notice how beneficial it is.

Exercise:

What I like about myself

Now sit down and make a conscious list of all the things about yourself that you like. Pin or hang it up somewhere as a constant reminder of what is deep within you already, in your very core.

For example:

"I like my laughter and that I can see the beautiful and the good in everything…"

Praise yourself for everything you have mastered so far, and keep updating your list.

Do this for at least five minutes every day.

The bowl of light

The ancient Hawaiians believed that we are not people who occasionally have spiritual experiences, but rather we are spiritual beings who have experiences as humans. Each of us is an original, there will never be anyone like us anywhere on Earth. We were given specific powers and abilities at birth in order to be able to fulfill our unique destiny here. We each have something within us that no other human being on Earth has. We have a unique "medicine," a unique being, and we should remain originals, rather than becoming copies.

The more we appreciate our abilities and talents, our beauty and strength, the more they will flourish. The notion of an individual "medicine" can change your entire life. If there are no two people on Earth with the same talents and abilities, words like competition, envy, jealousy, and comparison lose all meaning. Leading a fulfilled life means living according to your medicine, your destiny. There is enough for everyone; energy flows eternally.

A beautiful Hawaiian tradition

Every child that is born receives a bowl carved by a Hawaiian elder; it represents the bowl, filled with pure, divine, sacrosanct light, given at birth to every child for its path through life. This light is our happiness, our elixir of life. The bowl contains our gifts and abilities as well as the spiritual greatness that is placed within us. All human beings carry such spiritual greatness within themselves; they shine and their light illuminates the world.

During the course of our lives we invariably accumulate more and more experiences that block our light (for example, when we feel humiliated or life does not turn out the way we might have hoped). This is like *pohaku* (rocks or stones) falling into the bowl of light and preventing us from shining and shimmering as brightly in our unique spiritual greatness.

The Hawaiians have a simple solution for this. Each evening before sundown, they take their bowl of light and turn it upside down, emptying it of everything that has collected in the bowl during the day and allowing the light to shine and shimmer.

There are two kinds of *pohaku* that can displace or suppress the light of happiness. Each represents a troubling thought through which we give power over our happiness to something outside ourselves.

LILI is a thought that suggests a shortcoming of some kind and prevents us from being satisfied. It generally begins with the words: "Oh, if only I had…" *NINI* is the thought that other people are happier than we are and usually begins: "If only I were like…"

Happiness can be restored by a spiritual ally and by emptying the bowl. We accept everything the way life presents it to us. We see the blessing of the moment and follow the power that is within us. It will automatically guide us to happiness.

Exercise:
Emptying your individual bowl

Breathe in through your crown chakra and out through your navel. Repeat the exercise three times, finding your center, fully becoming yourself and connecting with yourself. Now take the feeling deep inside your heart. If it had a face, how would it look at you? How is your inner light? Now feel your bowl of light. In your imagination, take the bowl from within you, curl your hands into the shape of a bowl in front of your heart. How does that feel? What has collected in the bowl over the course of the

day? Taking a deep, powerful breath, empty the bowl over the ocean of light (quantum sea) and feel how the light energy transforms its contents in a split second. Now how do you feel? Put the bowl back within you and feel your heart, the eternal light of your Self. Allow it to spread out with every breath you take. Thank yourself for everything you dealt with successfully during the day and see the blessings in all the day's events and encounters.

In addition to our individual bowl of light, we also have a collective bowl in which we carry the stored issues that relate to our backgrounds, our ancestors, and the people with whom we are linked, consciously or unconsciously.

Feel the collective bowl in the vicinity of your navel, your second chakra. This is where everything from the collective unconscious accumulates; if we fail to keep an eye on it, it can make us helpless, sluggish, sick, and powerless.

Having worked intensively with these bowls, I can tell you that they can feel very different from one day to another. Sometimes they are buoyant, filled with light and sound, but at other times they are filled with heavy stones. It all depends on what has strayed into our energy fields during the day.

If you are doing this exercise for the first time, you may feel a need to wash the bowl of light in the ocean of love or to polish it after emptying. You can also ask your angels to do this; just trust the impulses you feel during this exercise.

Exercise:
Emptying the collective bowl

Allow your feelings to flow into the area of your stomach beneath your navel. Breathe in through your crown chakra and out through your navel. Repeat this exercise three times, finding your center, fully becoming and connecting with yourself. Lay your hands on your lower stomach and be fully aware of yourself. Focus entirely on being present in the moment. Feel the bowl of the collective consciousness within you. Now, in your imagination, remove the bowl from your stomach by curling your hands into the shape of a bowl in front of your stomach. How does the bowl feel? How does it smell? How do you perceive it and its contents?

Taking a deep breath, empty the bowl into the ocean of light energy, where its contents are transformed in a split second.

Take time with your bowl and, with the aid of your spirits (angels, masters, and power animals), think about what is needed to create its luster and achieve its ringing tone, allowing you to send healing impulses into the collective energy field. Place the bowl back within yourself and take a moment to enjoy the feeling; you will usually feel free, light, and full of energy after this exercise.

Practice this exercise every evening before you go to bed and you will be amazed at how different the results can be.

The bowl sometimes contains a message, a sign, a symbol, or a gift from our light-filled ancestors or sometimes from the collective consciousness.

Our light-filled ancestors

The true potential of our ancestors

Since the ancestors in our lineage have not been honored in our religion for many years and were often confronted with adversities in their era, we have forgotten where we come from, who we are, and what potential lies dormant within our lineage.

All the masters of time and space, every divinity that we know today, and countless nameless wise men and healers have lived on this planet and walked the Earth in the fullness of their power and greatness. It is important for us to become entirely who we are. Gautama Buddha is not Jesus Christ. Kuan Yin is not Mary Magdalene. Each master of light, of either gender, has their own very special vibration and consummately embodies their own very special power. All we have to do is be entirely ourselves and become ever more ourselves.

We often know something about the family members who have gone before us, perhaps going back as far as three or four generations, but in reality there are tens of thousands of souls standing behind these ancestors, spreading out across the branches of our family tree. Let us now widen our perspective and open ourselves up to our ancestral lineage. There was once a time when its true power was consciously passed on to us by our ancestors, and in some indigenous peoples it is still the case that certain powers and qualities are passed on from mothers and fathers to their children and to their children's children; this stream of potential can therefore continue to flow ever further.

It is now time for you to regain your true potential and allow it to awaken within the cells of your body. This will involve broadening your perspective. Here we offer you the opportunity to make contact with the potential of your six direct forebears.

Aligning with your six direct forebears

To begin, prepare a place in the room, perhaps on a circular rug or carpet, or a circle with a chair or a beanbag placed within it. Your mother and her parents are standing behind you to the left, and your father and his parents are to the right. Light a candle on the left side for your mother and on the right for your father, then a candle for your maternal grandfather and grandmother (even if you never knew them). Repeat the procedure for your father's parents (again, it does not matter if you knew them or not).

Sit down in your place and feel the six ancestors (your parents and grandparents) standing behind you. First be aware of your own position; it is often the case that we are not in the correct place in our family tree, or are drawn into a position that is unoccupied or not properly filled. It could be that we are standing in the position of one of our parents or other relatives, perhaps of a child who died. It is useful to first draw your family tree and ask yourself exactly where your position within it might be. Where is your exclusive place in your ancestors' family tree?

(Research a sample family tree online.)

Take your time with this preparatory work; it may bring you some insights. We often take on responsibility for people in our families (siblings, parents, grandparents, and so on) that we are really not obliged to bear. Or perhaps other relatives have taken on responsibility for us (siblings, aunts, uncles, and so on) because there was no other option.

If you have a godfather, be aware of this connection too, as it is special from an energy perspective.

Once you are fully aware of your place within the family tree, stand firmly in your allocated place. Allow yourself to feel only this position. Breathe your energy back in from all the other places where you took on something or bore something for someone else until you feel you have reached your place, calmly and peacefully. Thank those who took responsibility for you for a certain time and release them; take what is rightfully yours, you can now be there for yourself.

Feel your own very special connection to the Earth. Try imagining this link to the planet as a root anchored with seams of gold or silver, or with minerals or the elements. Allow a positive image to form within you, through which you feel the nurturing, supporting strength of Mother Earth for you, your life, and your unique path, wherever you are. It is always the same Earth beneath your feet, the Earth with which you are connected, which supports you and nurtures you for as long as you walk upon it. Only you can follow your unique path here, step by step. Your starting place is where your roots lie.

You are responsible only for this place and for all that has come from you (for example, children). Nothing else. In this exercise, it is also good to create order and peace for yourself and to see your children in their own unique places, and to bless them. If you sense empty places, ask the angels to bring healing to them too.

When you have taken your place, turn to your ancestors.

Picture the lines of ancestors standing behind you. Turn to face your ancestors and look at them.

Which of your ancestral lines do you feel most connected with?
    With which of them do you feel the least empathy?
    Take your time to explore each line with your feelings.

Many generations ago in your lineage, masters of light and ancestors developed their fullest potential and lived here on Earth as a child, or as a wife, lover, mother, spiritual teacher, priestess, healer, or as a man, lover, father, spiritual teacher, leader, priest, healer, or similar.

This potential has been handed down from generation to generation like a baton in a race.

There are *sleepers* in our lineage, ancestors who were unable to live out this potential but still passed it on, and *wakers*, ancestors who accessed this potential to the full.

The baton is now in your hand and it is up to you whether you are able to awaken your potential. If so, then not one life of your ancestors was in vain, and much healing and liberation can take place among the ranks of your forebears.

Meditation journey

Make yourself comfortable and take a few calm, deep breaths in and out. Dive deeper and deeper into the space of your heart, journey into yourself, and reach your very center. Now connect with the lineage and family tree of your tribe. Feel and see the place within it that is most essentially yours, that belongs only to you, and that only you can fill. Accept it now completely and entirely. Take some calming, deep breaths and transfer all your energy to this place. If there are any remnants of your energy in other places on the family tree, call them back to you in their entirety, and ask angels and beings from the unity of consciousness to fill the gaps and take up the places that have now become empty, so that you can stand in your place calmly, with clarity, and in peace.

See how the angels are now healing the wounds of your ancestors in the places where your energy was still present.

First, make a connection with your mother's ancestral lineage; feel your grandmother and all her ancestors. Breathe softly, calmly, and deeply.

Now ask your spirit guide to join you at your side. This might be an angel, a power animal, a master of either gender. Once you feel your guide's presence or know it is there, greet it in your own way.

You are now being brought to a boat, allowing yourself to be carried back in time down your ancestral lineage. The boat is being steered by your inner, sentient guide. You journey far back into the past, but no matter what you see or perceive on the banks of your ancestral lineage, the journey continues without stopping until you reach an ancestor who has achieved her fullest greatness and strength. You carry on further and further into the light. This ancestor has been waiting for you for a very long time. She may even be from another country, since you have no knowledge of your ancient origins. Marvel at what she shows you and accept it gratefully in your heart.

Your ancestor greets you entirely in love and takes you in her arms. She shows you the potential and the true power of your grandmother's ancestral lineage. Are you ready to accept this potential again in its entirety, its magnitude, and its power? If so, say: "Yes, I am ready."

Feel how this potential is now actuated in the very DNA of your body's cells and allow it to activate. All the old pain still stored within you flows away and is transformed in the light of your powerful potential.

Curl your hands into the shape of a bowl in front of your heart. Your ancestor sees you in possession of your full potential and with all her love hands to you a gift that belongs in your ancestral line.

It may be a color, object, symbol, energy, ceremony, ability, or simply some words that you hear; allow it to happen.

Wait until you can feel or see this gift very clearly and are aware of it; are you ready to accept it?

If you are ready and can feel the gift in your hands, place it on your heart and breathe it deep inside you. Feel how everything is activated within you.

Your ancestor may show you something else, initiate you into something, or have another message for you. It is now time to say farewell, in the knowledge that you and your ancestor can visit this place at any time in order for you to learn from or be guided by her. Give thanks for everything it was possible to make happen.

Now join your spiritual guide in climbing back into the boat and let yourself be transported back up your ancestral line to your place. Observe what is happening on the shores of your lineage as you return in your new, powerful vibration, with the full power of your ancestor's blessing behind you.

When you are fully back in your place once more, sit erect in your new strength and greatness.

You will feel the contact that has been made between you and your light-filled ancestor. A stream of blessings is beginning to pulse through your lineage, becoming ever stronger and more powerful. Many ancestors from your line can now go into the light completely, experiencing healing and liberation since their potential has been activated. Feel the liberation now taking place.

The stream slowly subsides and you return fully to yourself. Look at your spiritual guide one more time, give thanks, and anchor this strength to your inner self; feel how it is changing, how new places and paths are being created in perfect harmony with this reactivated strength.

Ask if there is anything else that should be addressed. Give thanks and let the blessing that comes from eternity radiate out into your spiritual space. Take slow breaths from your inner space into the outer room, returning to the here and now.

You can take the same journey to the ancestral line of your maternal grandfather and grandmother and your paternal grandfather.

Make a note of what you experienced in your meditation.

It is a way of learning a great deal about yourself, the true power of your ancestors and the potential that lies within you. From now on, it will protect, support, and guide you.

Our wise ancestors are often helpful teachers, guides, healers, and givers of good advice, who we can visit at any time, or they may suddenly appear during meditation when something important is about to happen. They have waited many eons for us to connect with them again.

You will also discover clear signs in your daily life and can ask for these at any time. Objects that you have seen in your meditation might be given to you as gifts, or you might be led to people who reconnect you with your power, or you might feel drawn to a particular country linked with your most ancient ancestors. Whenever you need strength and protection, you can also use these symbols and objects in your everyday life.

The insights that we gain from meditation may completely transform our lives.

Using the potential of your ancestors means that you are in a position to change shadow into light; everything is ready within you.

May peace and healing come your way, and may we rediscover the miracle of eternal life and the miracle that we ourselves are.

Meditation:
The healing look of love

Take a few deep breaths and be aware of your body. Feel the ground that supports you, giving you solidity and security. Let your eyes sink back into their sockets like a soft cushion and simply relax.

Consciously seek out your connection with the divine by opening your crown chakra and connecting with the heart of God, the source of Creation. Allow divine love to surround you and let all the light-beings that belong to you now come near: your light family, the angels and masters with whom you share a connection, your power animals. Sense how they surround you and look down on you with unconditional love.

And now, whatever your experience in life may have been with your parents and your ancestors, allow yourself to look into these loving eyes.

Breathe in this love and relax a little more into the experience of being seen by divine love. This love has no expectations, it is benevolent and watchful, awake and in the moment, tender and benign, and sees you as you really are.

Invite your light-filled ancestors to come here too, to give you gifts, to bring you strength, and to bless you.

Let yourself feel the light that is shone upon you. Feel the gaze of your light-filled ancestors; they are looking upon you as only loving parents can look at their children, proud of the path you have taken, empathizing with all the difficult times you have experienced, and full of joy that you remember your true being and that you are taking more and more of your light within you and are living it.

Remind yourself: I am light, I was always light, and I will be light for eternity; this light can shine in the world. Now bring yourself back to the present with a few deep breaths and, if you wish, light a candle as a visible symbol of the light within you.

OUR
SPIRITUAL
ANCESTORS

Aumakua—the lineage of our spirit ancestors

The word "OHANA" (family) means much more in the Hawaiian language than simply the line of descent of our forebears, the lineage of our father and mother. Family also includes our ancestors from previous incarnations, those who were on this planet in their full greatness and power many years ago, our cosmic parents, and our emotional and spiritual family, to whom we are deeply bound in our hearts. We may have experienced nonhuman incarnations, perhaps among the natural spirits, in the animal, plant, or mineral kingdoms, or in the angelic realms, cosmic domains, and stellar spheres. These incarnations can also be included among the ancestors with whom we are connected and who watch over us from the spiritual worlds.

In Huna everything is one and we are all related to everything. Prayers in shamanism often end with "for all my family," which includes all the living creatures in Creation and everything with which we are overtly and covertly connected.

An exercise with your spiritual ancestors

Ask yourself: "In which realms does my soul feel at home?"
Among the Aumakua spiritual realms are the following:
  Elements: fire, water, earth, air, ether
  Natural realm: dwarves, fairies, elves, pixies, mermaids, nixies, fire beings…
  Plant realm: Elves, flower fairies, dancers

Mineral realm: watchers, protectors, energy keepers, stored memories, crystal beings

Animal realm: animals that you particularly like

Awakened humans: spiritual teachers, kahunas, priesthoods, monks, yogis, druids, medicine men or women, shamans, healers, herbalists, witches, magicians, alchemists, secret orders, storytellers, traveling entertainers

Countries: countries that hint at ancient knowledge in your soul (Greece, Egypt, Central America, Africa)

Angelic realm: angels, archangels, Seraphim, Elohim

Spiritual areas: Shambhala, Avalon, Egyptian mystery schools, Atlantis, Lemuria…

Stellar beings: Pleiades, Sirius, Orion, Mars, Venus, the Moon, Jupiter, other solar systems

Reconnect with your spirit lineage and allow that ancient knowledge to be reawakened. Invite your Aumakua to spiritual celebrations, ceremonies, and sessions. Visit them in your inner spiritual space via meditations, shamanic journeys, and similar. They will strengthen and guide you in your own unique way.

Writing exercise:
Remembrance

Find a piece of paper and a pen or pencil and sit down. Wait until you are feeling calm and breathe in the light of your soul.

With which realms do you feel most deeply connected?

What experiences have you most encountered in your life?

Which places are you repeatedly drawn to?

Which animals, plants, and parts of the countryside do you love in particular?

Allow all your connections to the non-human, spiritual, and emotional realms to rise within you.

Eye exercise:
Seeing the potential and strength in others

Perform this exercise with another person. Sit opposite one another and look into each other's eyes with the aim of bringing out your spirit lineage. Simply watch as your partner opens up and inwardly connects with their potential.

Which realms, what strengths do you perceive in the person sitting opposite you?

Their face may change and take on different expressions during the exercise. You might perhaps see an angel, priestess, or animal. You might see the face of an ancient Indian or Tibetan, or perceive something not of this world, an elf, mermaid, or fairy. Allow this to take place without judgment.

Observe what happens silently for around five minutes, while music plays or a drum is gently beaten. You can also close your eyes occasionally to receive spiritual impressions. Look for the soul potential, strength, and realms that you can identify in the person facing you. Swap notes, and then swap roles.

Accept the strength of your soul and allow your potential to awaken. Forces as yet undreamt of slumber within our spirit ancestors' lineage and will help you to recognize, accept, and carry out any mission you may have as a builder of bridges between these worlds. Focus on the realms from which parts of your soul are descended; get to know them in your inner space and learn from them.

Aumakua-Spirit-Family Meditation

IN CONTACT WITH THE ORIGIN OF OUR SOUL'S SPIRITUAL PARENTS—OUR TRUE HOME

In addition to our earthly origins, we also have a spiritual source. Alongside our human existence, many of us have spiritual roots in other realms and kingdoms. These might be the natural, angelic, or stellar realms, the mineral kingdom, or your soul's ancient home. Making contact with our true home helps us to recognize ourselves and to finally be able to mirror ourselves in what we truly are. It is an awakening to our true being.

Meditation

Make sure you feel comfortable. Concentrate on your breathing and take a few deep breaths.

Breathe in through your crown chakra and out through your navel. Repeat this exercise three times.

You are gradually sinking down from your conscious understanding through your neck into the space of your heart. Allow this space to become broader, brighter, and larger. You notice an entrance. It might lead to a cave, tunnel, gate, corridor, or something similar. You go through it. A path lies before you leading to a place where you feel completely safe and secure. As you walk along this path, you open your inner senses.

Walk around your inner space and begin to explore it. What plants and trees grow there? What scenery do you see?

What animals do you meet? Is your inner space laid out like a garden or does it grow wild? Is the soil fertile? Does the space radiate power and energy? Are there any small areas that could be cleaned or changed? Where do the paths lead? Enjoy discovering more and more about this inner space.

The inner center—orientation

A powerful wave of energy is drawing you gently but firmly ever closer to your inner center, your core. This represents a very special focus in your inner space. There may be a stone or crystal there, a strong, special tree, or a spring, or perhaps even a temple. Be especially aware of your inner core. How do the elements of fire, water, earth, and air feel? How does the energy flow here? What aura and which qualities are in the inner core? You notice how you are beginning to connect with everything here and to expand. You are aware of the ground beneath your feet and the place where you are standing.

As you take your next breath, stretch forward, and then with another breath, reach backward. Stretch left and right with each next successive breath. Finally, take another breath, stretch upward, and connect with your higher being. Beams of luminous light now flow from the higher dimensions into your being, so that you feel completely reinvigorated.

Ask your spirits to join you. Helpful beings, such as a power animal, angel, master, healer, and natural being, or an entire group of beings begin to reveal themselves. Greet them and get to know them. They will support and accompany you at an inner level.

Preparing to return home

From the center of your being, a path appears that leads to a place of preparation. Your spirits accompany you along the path and you reach a magical place where crystal-clear water bubbles up, lit by beams of radiant light. This water is the water of eternal life. Cast off all that is old and immerse yourself in the water.

It has a healing and cleansing effect. It flows into you and through you. Your spiritual guides remove things from your body that should not be there, and you feel old wounds beginning to heal and toxins leaving your body.

You feel lighter and purer with every breath as you return to the energy of innocence. Bathe in this cleansing, pure energy, enjoy your innocent, divine being. Breathe in and out; you are diving down into the water and can sense that a great initiation into the spiritual world is about to take place.

Eventually, it is time for you to get out of the water. You are welcomed, anointed, oiled, and prepared for your homecoming. You are given a gown that is attuned to the frequency of your energy vibration. You are now ready for your true, spiritual home.

Initiation

A path now appears from your center that leads to one of the Earth's ancient holy places, one you have not visited and yet know well, a place where you can connect with your true home. Your spirits accompany you there. You look around, breathing in deeply, and they ask you whether you are ready to connect with your origins. Slowly and carefully, you approach the place that you came from, feeling the traces of light that you leave behind with every step as you venture ever further into your holiest inner being. It is as if an invisible gate is opening and you are being drawn further and further toward your true spiritual home, into the realm from which your soul once emerged (Nature, the inner Earth, angels, Akasha, your homeworld in the stars…).

A shimmering point of light in the distance is approaching, getting ever closer. It is like the light at the end of a tunnel. You see your spiritual home. Many beings are already there waiting for you. What is the landscape like? What colors, shapes, and energies are shining to greet you? Finally you arrive. You touch the ground of your spiritual home. Many beings, all of whom are well known to you, greet and welcome you.

Deeply moved, you let them embrace and welcome you. At last.

A sound is heard and the beings move aside to form a path. At the end stand two shining figures in shimmering gowns: your spiritual father and your spiritual mother. You move toward these beings, and upon reaching them, you look into their loving eyes. It is as if you are recognizing yourself for the first time, and you know: I AM HOME, THIS IS WHERE I BELONG. You look at your spiritual mother, she takes you in her arms and cradles you, glad that you have returned. As she does this, you feel all the old images of her fall away from you and your soul breathes a deep sigh of relief. Then you look into the loving eyes of your spiritual father. Here you can find yourself again. He embraces you and rocks you back and forth, and you feel all the old images, beliefs, and identities melting away; you feel your soul sigh. The love of your spiritual parents surrounds and warms you; you feel how every scrap of this love from which you were created is filled with vital energy.

Your spiritual parents now ask you to accompany them. You ask how long you were separated from this place and they tell you. They lead you to your true home. You enter a wonderful building that you already know intimately, perhaps from your dreams and visions.

Yes, this is your home.

Your spiritual parents take you to your space in the building. You look around. All your talents, abilities, qualities, and true characteristics have been carefully stored here, untouched and undamaged. As you walk around, you begin to remember. You take certain objects and pictures in your hands and old memories rise to the surface, old abilities are awakened. You feel the frequency of your ancient resonance awakening within you, and you are glad that everything has been preserved. Take your time!

In full knowledge that you will return here later, your spiritual parents ask you to follow them. They lead you into an inner temple where many beings that have been connected with you in some way over the ages have gathered. As you walk through the crowd, you feel the different emotions, both resolved and unresolved, you feel the conflicts and disputes, the connections and links, and free-flowing energy. Sense the energy field with which you are still connected to this day. How does it feel? Who is there?

Your parents lead you to the place of transformation, where you will find the water of eternal life, pure, clear, luminous, and unadulterated. As you gaze into these calm waters, they begin to move gently. Many lives, and different roles and situations reveal themselves in the water, scrolling past you as though in a film. You feel how the masks you have worn and the roles you have played over the years are falling away and you are becoming more and more what you really were, are, and will be once again. You are transforming ever more into your true self, the self that lies behind all the roles, masks, and incarnations; you are beginning to discover yourself. Your image is becoming clearer, purer, younger, brighter, and more beautiful. You can feel this change and transformation within you. Look yourself in the eye. What radiates out toward you? You are enjoying just being yourself; breathe in deeply and allow this transformation to take place. You are.

You now turn around. All the beings gathered here across time and space have shared in the experience of your transformation. You are now showing yourself as you really are. A recognition and an awakening are taking place. The energy field is beginning to dissolve and to clear in harmony with your true vibration. Some of the beings are celebrating and are so happy that you have returned, while others are greeting you or asking for forgiveness. Others still are experiencing a moment of

93

grace, detaching easily and effortlessly from your energy field, floating away like clouds into the sky. New beings are entering the space and invite you in; your energy field feels peaceful, light, buoyant, and harmonious. You are glad.

Your spiritual parents and the beings that are bound to you in joy and love take you by the hand and lead you to a special place that has long been prepared and safeguarded for you. Only you have the key to this place. It is linked with your birth crystal, your original energy. You are brought to the entrance, and from there you carry on alone, softly and slowly advancing deeper and deeper into the crystalline energy of your origins as it opens up to you, as if by its own volition. You dive completely into your own original energy, feeling it fully activated in the cells of your body. Enjoy it; feel your primal pattern, your original aura, your original energy in every cell, every atom. You are becoming complete, fully charged with energy.

It is now time to leave this holy place that has been safeguarded for you.

Completely fulfilled and recharged with energy, you are brought back to your space. Your parents remind you why you once came to Earth. What did you wish to bring the Earth? What is your task? They ask you whether you are ready to complete this mission and what it is that you have most lacked until this moment. You answer. Now you can receive from your space what has most been missing and what you need in order to best complete your work. Your spiritual parents place it in your energy field and anchor this

vibration there. You feel yourself opening up in their presence, full of love and trust, sensing what has been lacking and what you need being anchored there. Explore your energy field and your new vibration.

You look around your space one more time. Safe in the knowledge that this connection has been reestablished and you can return to the place of your origin at any time, you feel ready to bring your mission on Earth to completion.

Your spiritual parents lead you back to the departure point. You look deep into your spiritual mother's eyes. She gives you a gift for your feminine side and takes you tenderly in her arms. You look deeply into your spiritual father's eyes. He hands you a gift for your masculine side and cradles you in all his love. You feel how the masculine and feminine sides within you are healed in this love. You are a divine child experiencing life on Earth and are connected with the original

energy of your being. Your spiritual parents may tell you its name or how it resonates. You feel their blessing and the light of love that will surround you and be with you from now on. Showered in gifts and blessings, you are ready to return.

A gate opens and you are drawn back automatically to the holy ground where your journey began. Once you have arrived, you slowly approach the place where your spirits are waiting, rejoicing at the change within you; they welcome you.

You follow the path back to your inner core. Once there, you anchor your original energy to your inner place. As you set foot there, it begins to change and to realign itself completely. Watch as this takes place and experience the transformation.

Perhaps a new space is being created, becoming lighter and broader. New paths of love are forming.

Observe and take pleasure in this inner transformation and reorientation. Look around you, bless this inner space, and step fully into your center. You allow your true original energy to expand, radiating throughout your body, transforming it entirely. You feel your old image falling away, every cell in your body becoming recharged and rejuvenated, as this energy starts to radiate out from your core to every world and dimension with which you are visibly and invisibly connected. You slowly breathe yourself back into the room in which you now find yourself. Take a moment to compose yourself and sense the new light glowing within you. Take your time, until you are back in the room completely.

From now on it is up to you to keep connecting with your true origins until the end of this time.

Completion and integration

Even when we have experienced many new and wonderful things, it is often not easy for our bodies to take everything in. The following journey will help you here.

Integration and blessing meditation

Make yourself comfortable. Be centered in yourself. Push everything that does not belong to you out of your energy field, passing it back through the violet fire of transformation to those to whom it belongs. Now place these people in God's hands. Finally, breathe your energies completely back into your body.

Imagine that you are once more entirely consciously slipping into your body, as if into a glove, so that your consciousness fills your entire body to the tips of your fingers and toes. Consciously allow your foot chakras to open up in trust to the light of the Earth and the loving, nurturing power of the Great Mother, the Great Goddess.

Now sense how she touches you, the Great Goddess who in her core is always loving, nurturing, and awakened … she provides you with all the regenerative energy you need. Breathe in this nurturing life force from beneath you through your feet, drawing it up into your body as you breathe in, just as the roots of a tree draw up water. Spread it throughout your entire body as you breathe out.

Remember that life nourishes you and that you do not have to do anything to accept this life force naturally, that it is given in love so that you can fully live your light and your potential.

Feel how you are enveloped by a field of light from above, how your light family is moving toward you, how you are surrounded by divine love. Your light family has now come to accompany you to a temple of integration, remembrance, and awakening.

Your angel or spirit guide now takes you by the hand and leads you along a very special path to your temple of integration. You see it before you, luminous, sparkling, and shimmering. You sense this light touch your heart, which you feel swell and open, and you enter the temple with your angel and your light family. Inside, you are led to a welcoming seat where you make yourself comfortable once more.

Here in this temple you need do nothing, you can simply be … and receive.

You sense your light family gathered around you, along with the angels, masters, and all the light-filled beings from other realms that belong to you, who look down upon you lovingly and touch your body and your aura wherever you need support.

You sense how your spiritual ancestors emerge and once again completely surround you with the frequency of your spiritual home, the home from which you come and in which you have lived out your awakened potential in some previous time. There may be some surprises, different lineages from among your spiritual ancestors may appear.

Sense how your ancestors now flood you with the very special light of this awakened lineage, how your body is filled with it, entering every cell in your body, and how your DNA is once more harmonizing with your highest spiritual vibration. Your highest potential is awakening; you breathe gently and give yourself over to it.

Now you sense how your four light-filled ancestors step out from your father and your mother's lineage in their highest potential. See how they stand in their full light. They too are now allowing this shining light to flow into your body through their hands, reminding you that all this is your heritage, activating your whole body with your utmost potential.

Feel how your cells now vibrate for a moment, how these lines of light from the different highest potentials form inside you as if in a completely new dance of your very own. Feel how your cells begin to shine, how the stream of love from which you originate is reawakened in your whole being—in your spirit, your soul, and here in your body, in your human form.

Your light-filled ancestors from your genetic and spiritual lineage assure you once more that you can call on them at any time, that they are always there to support you, strengthening your resolve. They lift their hands in blessing. Open yourself to their love, their benevolence, and their blessing now, so that you can awaken in your true greatness.

Now rise from the seat in the temple of integration and stand fully in your own light, broad and filled with dignity, and in the full knowledge of who you are … a divine consciousness collecting experiences here on Earth … in a human body.

Remember that you are also here to reawaken the consciousness of love on this planet, in the knowledge of who you are.

Your ancestors now accompany you to a very special altar, where you see the gifts of your soul; they are a long since forgotten part of you. Look at everything that belongs to you. What wealth, what riches!

Let yourself breathe in the light frequency of these gifts, inviting their energy into you even though you may not yet know what to do with them. Take everything you need, all the seeds that may one day bloom within you, in your heart; say yes to yourself and to your uniqueness, your richness.

You can return to this temple whenever you like and whenever you feel the need to remember, regenerate, or to rest. Your spiritual guide will return to your side and you can meet them, as an equal, a light-being encountering a light-being. You will then be gently led back out of the temple of integration into this space. Consciously bring all your light here into your body, into the temple of your soul.

Take a few breaths a little more deeply than usual in order to come back completely into the present moment.

Allow yourself a little more time to rest.

Reverberation

TESTIMONIALS BY
ANCESTOR WORK SEMINAR PARTICIPANTS

I feel very peaceful after the process. I entered a larger energy field and was able to use it to send many blessings into the energy fields in which I had previously been caught up. I feel as if I have freed myself and can now follow my own path. I am filled with peace and gratitude.

I feel very supported and secure after this process. A great deal of healing has taken place within me and I have strength, new joy, and have found new confidence in life and in the fulfillment of my tasks. I feel great benevolence from my ancestors. Thank you.

I felt such warmth at my back when my ancestors suddenly appeared there behind me, and I realized that I am no longer alone. They were all delighted to see me. Many thanks.

I really take after my mother and her side of the family as far as my appearance is concerned. I found it amazing and deeply moving that the ancestral line of my dear paternal grandmother reaches back to the lineage of my spiritual ancestors in Atlantis, and that there is something that has been, is, and always will be so deep and so nourishing.

I sensed that there is no separation between our genetic and spiritual ancestors. We are one.

Thank you for the love, the strength, the consolation, and the transformation that I was privileged to experience. The transformation process was much deeper than I could have imagined and I have a new awareness of all the ancestors and the powers that stand behind me and look down upon me with love.

I came home here and that was a great gift for me. I am deeply moved and full of gratitude.

I used to have such arguments with my parents and for such a long time. After carrying out the "finding peace with your parents" meditation I was suddenly able to see them in a new light, with so much more empathy, and I have a much better understanding of so much. I feel much more reconciled with them.

Afterword by Jeanne Ruland

In your generation, in your time, your life's work is not far away. Your parents gave you the gift of life and everything else they gave you was a blessing. Give thanks for this and move forward along your path, cheerfully and happily, full of joy and peace.

Everything you need is within you. You can never escape yourself. Your "medicine," talents, and abilities will guide you from within.

> *This is where love lives, this is where the light shines that heralds a new day.*

Awaken in your true inheritance—accept these powers again. The stars are watching over you, they will truly guide you on your path. Aumakua, you who came before me and cleared my path, I bless you and I listen with my heart. May the old pain be healed.

May we awaken in light and laugh once more together. Thank you for your eternal guidance, vigilance, and the light within, for the transformation and healing that takes place when we finally see you again.

Our goal is to recognize our inheritance and to find a new name for our strengths.

Afterword by Shantidevi

I follow my path, I sense your loving, light-filled eyes upon me, deeply benevolent, encouraging, and strengthening. I follow the call of my heart and grow into the love that you —Aumakua— have long since entered into. I feel your blessing and share my treasures and my heritage with the world.

Although often long hidden behind the veil of forgetfulness, the light-filled heritage of our ancestors and our souls dwells within us. It awakens within us, little by little, and flows back into our lives once again. When we are seen as we really are, when we have affirmation and are encouraged to be entirely ourselves, connections for new, joyful experiences are created in our brains. We finally become what we have always been in our deepest being, a divine consciousness in human form.

An endless stream of blessings flows from this consciousness into our lives and the lineage of our family, forward to our children and backward to our ancestors. By being ourselves, we encourage others to free themselves from old patterns of behavior and entanglements. May we all remember who we really are and give our loving uniqueness and enthusiasm as a gift to the world. Our light-filled ancestors are looking down on us with love and are blessing our path.

About the authors

Jeanne Ruland is the mother of three children, an author with many years of training in shamanism and metaphysics, a Huna teacher, and a recognized healer within the "Spiritual Healing" umbrella organization. She has now amassed a wealth of experience in dealing with the spiritual powers that  lead to unity, God, the Source, and the self that is within the core of everyone. She has encountered many spiritual masters and forces on her journeys and has completed a range of different training courses. By the time she felt a vocation to write, she had acquired a wealth of practical experience and knowledge in which Heaven and Earth are connected. She began to write books and to give seminars in the year 2000. Her first works were *The Light Power of Angels* and *The Big Book of Angels* and, like all her books, card sets, and calendars, these were published by Schirner Verlag. Jeanne Ruland loves to share the knowledge of her heart with people through her books and in lectures, seminars, and workshops, helping to guide others toward themselves and the source of strength within them.

Further information is available at: www.shantila.de

Shantidevi Cornelia Felgenhauer has been an alternative healer with her own practice since 1989, specializing in spiritual psychotherapy, family system work, and trauma work using Peter Levine's methodology, as well as reincarnation therapy. She encountered the angels and masters who  guide her and teach her at an early point on her spiritual path. She finds great joy in accompanying people on their own paths, helping them to unlock their fullest potential, leave the shadow of their past behind, and finally to make peace with what once was and is now. With all her heart, she helps people to remember that we come from love and that we are love. She shares the treasures that she has found along her path in individual sessions and, since 1991, in groups and seminars as well. She has published ten meditation CDs and books.

Further information is available at: www.shantidevi.de

Picture credits

Decorative designs

Ornaments p. 3: kurbanov; floral border: MyStocks; small blossom: Sunset And Sea Design; masks p. 23: pixaroma; DNA p. 29: Anita Ponne; sea turtle p. 83: Katja Gerasimova. All shutterstock.com

Photography

Page 8: Fominayaphoto; 13: iMoStudio; p. 24: David G Hayes; p. 27: orxy; p. 32: fizkes; p. 37: Romrodphoto; p. 39, p. 49: Kaya Shelest; p. 40: Monkey Business Images; p. 44: Christin Lola; p. 56: Tom4u; p. 63: Dmytro Zinkevych; p. 69, p. 71, p. 103: Jeanne Ruland; p. 73: Srah Photography; p. 77: youli zhao; p. 81: Shantidevi; p. 85: Shane Myers Photography; p. 87: Fominayaphoto; p. 95: Dean Pennala; p. 102: Prystai; p. 108: Supavadee butradee. All shutterstock.com

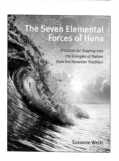

Susanne Weikl
The Seven Elemental Forces of Huna
Practices for Tapping into the Energies of
Nature from the Hawaiian Tradition
Paperback, full-color throughout, 128 pages
ISBN 978-1-62055-885-0

Huna is an ancient shamanic tradition from Hawaii that recognizes seven elemental Nature powers into which we can tap anywhere and at any time. Connect your soul with water, fire, wind, rock, plants, animals, and beings of light. The easy to implement exercises, techniques, and rituals presented in this book will enable you to draw on the strength of the natural forces for empowerment.

Shai Tubali
Unlocking the Seven Secret Powers
of the Heart
A Practical Guide to Living in Trust and Love
Paperback, full-color throughout, 128 pages
ISBN 978-1-62055-812-6

The heart, often perceived as our most vulnerable and fragile place, is in fact the source of our greatest potential. This book will unveil the seven secret powers of the heart and help you to discover how you can awaken them. This will lead you to a deep sense of peace, balance, and fulfillment and enable you to approach life from a place of trust and love.

Ulrich Emil Duprée
Ho'oponopono and Family Constellations
A traditional Hawaiian healing method for
relationships, forgiveness, and love
Paperback, full-color throughout, 160 pages
ISBN 978-1-84409-717-3

Both Ho'oponopono, the Hawaiian forgiveness ritual, and family constellation therapy help to heal our relationships with the world around us and bring healing to our inner world. This hands-on book brings together what belongs together, providing beginners with an introduction and easy access to the subject and the more experienced with fresh insights.

Ulrich Emil Duprée
Ho'oponopono
The Hawaiian forgiveness ritual as the key
to your life's fulfillment
Paperback, full-color throughout, 96 pages
ISBN 978-1-84409-597-1

Powerful yet concise, this revolutionary guide summarizes the Hawaiian ritual of forgiveness and offers methods for immediately creating positive effects in everyday life. Ho'oponopono consists of four consequent magic sentences: "I am sorry. Please forgive me. I love you. Thank you." By addressing issues using these simple sentences we get to own our feelings, and accept unconditional love, so that unhealthy situations transform into favorable experiences.

For further information and to request a book catalog contact:
Inner Traditions, One Park Street, Rochester, Vermont 05767

Earthdancer Books is an Inner Traditions imprint.
Phone: +1-800-246-8648, customerservice@innertraditions.com
www.earthdancerbooks.com • www.innertraditions.com

AN INNER TRADITIONS IMPRINT